ROCK & POP
Classics

Being with You
For intimate evenings and quiet nights

Being with You

This volume of *Rock & Pop Classics* brings together some of pop music's most sensual and seductive artists. Whether it is the angelic voice of Smokey Robinson crooning the title track or the tender harmonies of Extreme showing how it takes "More Than Words" to show you care, *Being with You* provides the ideal soundtrack for an evening at home with the one you love. We all want to be close to someone, secure in the comfort of a loving relationship. *Being with You* perfectly expresses those desires by way of some of music's most romantic duets, including Patti Austin and James Ingram's "Baby, Come to Me" and Eddie Rabbitt and Crystal Gayle's "You and I." So dim the lights and let yourself get swept away in the romantic possibilities of *Being with You*.

THE LISTENER'S GUIDE – WHAT THE SYMBOLS MEAN

THE INSPIRATION
The stories behind the music and artists

THE ARTIST
The lives, the loves... the scandal

THE MUSIC
Why songs sound the way they do

THE BACKGROUND
People, places and events that shape the songs

Contents

– 2 –
SMOKEY ROBINSON
Being with You

– 4 –
**GROVER WASHINGTON, JR.
AND BILL WITHERS**
Just the Two of Us

– 6 –
THE STYLISTICS
Betcha by Golly, Wow

– 8 –
BRENDA RUSSELL
Piano in the Dark

– 10 –
COMMODORES
Three Times a Lady

– 12 –
BOBBY CALDWELL
What You Won't Do for Love

– 14 –
CAPTAIN & TENNILLE
Do That to Me One More Time

– 16 –
DEBBIE GIBSON
Lost in Your Eyes

– 18 –
EXTREME
More Than Words

– 20 –
RITA COOLIDGE
We're All Alone

– 22 –
**EDDIE RABBITT AND
CRYSTAL GAYLE**
You and I

– 24 –
**PEABO BRYSON &
ROBERTA FLACK**
Tonight I Celebrate My Love

– 26 –
**PATTI AUSTIN
(A DUET WITH JAMES INGRAM)**
Baby, Come to Me

– 28 –
PEACHES & HERB
Reunited

ROCK & POP
Classics

Being with You
SMOKEY ROBINSON

A sparkling ballad about how love can conquer all, "Being with You" gave Smokey Robinson a No. 2 hit in 1981. Coming nearly 11 years after he had topped the chart with "The Tears of a Clown," this single proved that Robinson had lost none of his star power. His voice sounded as youthful as ever, with his breathy tenor used to perfection against tinkling electric piano chords and a warm, jazzy saxophone. "Being with You" once again proved that Robinson's reputation as the most successful creator of romantic soul music was well earned.

MIRACLE WORKER

After Robinson left his group, the Miracles, in 1972, neither was able to match the incredible success they had achieved during their collaboration. But the Miracles scored a No. 1 hit in 1976 with "Love Machine" and Robinson went on to enjoy several Top 10 hits on his own. Robinson had originally offered "Being with You," his highest-charting single, to Kim Carnes *(right)*. Ironically, it was Carnes' "Bette Davis Eyes" that kept Robinson's single from reaching the top spot.

WHERE THERE'S SMOKE...

Robinson met Motown founder Berry Gordy, Jr. in the 1950s, at a time when he was looking for a mentor and Gordy was looking for a visionary singer-songwriter. The two clicked and began one of the richest collaborations of all time. Although the Miracles *(left)* weren't Motown's biggest act, they were its most consistent, racking up an impressive 27 Top 40 hits during Robinson's tenure. And Robinson didn't stop performing miracles once he left the group—as vice president of Motown, he was instrumental in creating the sound that would launch countless careers.

NOT JUST A PRETTY VOICE

Born in Detroit, Mich., in 1940, William "Smokey" Robinson was dubbed "America's greatest living poet" by Bob Dylan in the mid-1960s. And this was not false praise. In addition to writing or cowriting several smash hits for the Miracles, including the No. 1 "The Tears of a Clown," Robinson also wrote some of the biggest singles in Motown history for other artists. Robinson's many songwriting credits include "My Guy" for Mary Wells *(left)*, who took the song to No. 1 in 1964, and several hits—including "My Girl" and "Get Ready"—for the Temptations.

Smokey with wife Claudette, who also performed with the Miracles from 1954 until '64.

KEY NOTES

Robinson's children's names reflect his love of soul music: Son Berry is named after Motown's Berry Gordy; his daughter's name, Tamla, comes from the Tamla-Motown label.

Just the Two of Us
GROVER WASHINGTON, JR. AND BILL WITHERS

This song brought together two seemingly disparate artists in jazz sax man Grover Washington, Jr. and soul singer Bill Withers. Taken from Washington's Grammy-winning *Winelight* album, "Just the Two of Us" reached No. 2 on the pop chart and No. 3 on the R&B chart in 1981. The song also earned a Grammy for Best R&B Song.

 ### SAMPLE MAN

Withers' smooth vocals are a perfect fit for this song—his first pop hit in almost a decade—which he cowrote. During the early '70s, Withers *(below)* had an incredible string of pop hits, including "Lean on Me," "Ain't No Sunshine" and "Use Me." He has not recorded much since the 1980s, preferring his partial retirement from the music business. But others have continued to tap into his music. His songs have been sampled for everything from rap songs to Gap commercials.

SAX APPEAL

Washington came from a musical family. His father played saxophone, his mother sang in a chorus and his brother played the drums. Young Grover first picked up the sax when was 10 years old. At 16, he left home to go on tour with a band called the Four Clefs. After a stint in the Army, he took to music full time. His session work in the early 1970s was impressive enough to get the attention of legendary producer Creed Taylor *(left)* who signed him to Kudu Records.

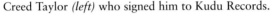

THE BEST OF ALL WORLDS

Washington caught the jazz fusion explosion at the right time, and his records, which blended jazz, pop and funk, found commercial success. From the mid-'70s to the early '80s, Washington had seven straight albums go to No. 1 on the jazz chart. He tried to remain true to his early influences, such as Dexter Gordon, Stanley Turrentine and Sonny Rollins *(right)*, but he also refused to stand still musically. "I would like to believe that some of the reason I've been around so long is that I don't do the same thing over and over," Washington once said. "I like to grow, to keep adding another thread to my musical tapestry. I'm just staying true to the things that got me to play in the first place."

KEY NOTES

In 1998, Will Smith (left) had a Top 20 hit with his remake of "Just the Two of Us," adding his own rap about the joys of being a father.

Washington scored the theme songs for two of the most popular TV shows of the '80s: The Cosby Show and Moonlighting (right).

Betcha by Golly, Wow

THE STYLISTICS

With its lush five-part harmonies, soulful rhythm track and the seductive falsetto of Russell Thompkins, Jr., this song was one of seven Top 20 hits for the Stylistics during a three-year period in the early 1970s.

"Betcha by Golly, Wow," which climbed to No. 3 in 1972, has been covered by several artists, including Johnny Mathis, Smokey Robinson & the Miracles and, most notably, the Artist formerly known as Prince.

SONGWRITERS' CREED

"Betcha by Golly, Wow" was written by two of the most important figures in the growth of Philly soul, Linda Creed and Thom Bell *(left)*. In the 1970s, Creed penned lyrics to numerous Thom Bell melodies, including hits for the Delfonics, Spinners and O'Jays—not to mention all of the Stylistics biggest hits. In 1977, Creed cowrote "Greatest Love of All," which later became a No. 1 hit for Whitney Houston. Creed died in 1986 after a long battle with breast cancer. She was inducted into the Songwriters Hall of Fame in 1992.

TWO FOR ONE

The Stylistics were a hybrid of two Philly vocal groups. In 1968, bass James Smith, tenor Airrion Love and falsetto Russell Thompkins, Jr. *(below)* of the Monarchs joined baritones Herb Murrell and James Dunn of the Percussions to form Herb and the Boys, who later became the Stylistics. Marty Bryant, another former Monarch, was the group's first manager and cowrote "You're a Big Girl Now," a local hit in Philadelphia in 1970. Avco Embassy Records took notice of the single and signed the group the following year.

HIGH NOTE

Like all of the Stylistics hits, "Betcha by Golly, Wow," from their self-titled debut album *(right)*, was a ballad that featured the mellow horns and sweet strings that were hallmarks of Philly soul. But it was Thompkins' captivating voice that stole the show. In fact, Avco Embassy Records even listed the group as "The Stylistics, featuring Russell Thompkins, Jr."

KEY NOTES

After the hits stopped coming in the U.S., the Stylistics found renewed success in the U.K., where The Best of the Stylistics became the top-selling album of 1975.

Piano in the Dark
BRENDA RUSSELL

Music has the power to make even the hardest heart melt, often despite the firmest resolution to resist. To hear her sing it, this is exactly what happens to Brenda Russell in "Piano in the Dark." This atmospheric ballad features Russell's soaring, emotional vocals against the romantic sound of a tinkling piano. Taken from her album *Get Here*, the song hit No. 6 in 1988.

 ## WRITE ON

In addition to singing with other artists, Russell writes for them as well. With more than 120 songs to her credit, she has had songs recorded by the likes of Roberta Flack and Luther Vandross *(left)*. Donna Summer had her biggest hit in three years with Russell's "Dinner with Gershwin" in 1987.

BIG NOISE

Russell's portfolio as a backup singer is impressive. Working with some of pop's biggest voices, she has more than held her own with women such as Barbra Streisand *(right)*, Dusty Springfield and Bette Midler—not to mention male artists including Elton John. When jazz group the Yellowjackets decided to record a version of Russell's song "Love and Paris Rain" in 1998, they could think of no better performer to sing it than Russell herself, which she willingly did.

 ## GOING IT ALONE

Born Brenda Gordon, Russell moved to Canada with her family when she was 12 years old. Growing up in Toronto, she met husband-to-be Brian Russell, and the pair went on to work as hosts of the Canadian TV series *Music Machine*. In 1973, they moved to Los Angeles and worked as session artists before recording together as Brian & Brenda. After their separation in 1978, Russell *(right)* began her more successful solo career.

KEY NOTES

In 1991, R&B singer Oleta Adams scored a Top 5 hit with a remake of the title track from Russell's Get Here *album.*

Three Times a Lady
COMMODORES

After hearing the Commodores' "Three Times a Lady," Lionel Richie's wife, Brenda—to whom the song was dedicated—must have been left with no doubt as to how Richie felt about her. Beginning with a gently murmuring piano that underscores Richie's sincere vocals, the track builds toward a shimmering crescendo of cymbals and heavenly harmonies. "Three Times a Lady" topped the chart in 1978, and became one of Motown's biggest sellers of the 1970s.

SOLO SURVIVOR

After writing and singing a string of hits with the Commodores, Lionel Richie began to pursue outside projects.

He wrote and produced Kenny Rogers' No. 1 hit "Lady" in 1980. The success of "Endless Love," his 1981 duet with Diana Ross *(above)*, convinced him to go solo. He went on to become one of the top-selling artists of the 1980s.

PERFECT EXPOSURE

The Commodores' career was given a huge boost in 1971 when Suzanne de Passe, creative vice president of Motown, hired them to support the Jackson 5 *(left)* on tour. As a result, they were seen by the children of Motown's

Berry Gordy, who insisted their father sign the band. The Commodores later supported the Rolling Stones on their world tour in 1975, which helped broaden their audience base even further.

AIMING FOR THE TOP

The Commodores were a soul band, but Richie longed to establish himself in a wider field: "As a songwriter, I never wanted to be the best R&B or country composer. I just wanted to be the best. I wanted to be classed with Stevie Wonder, Lennon and McCartney, Elton John and Bernie Taupin *(right)*. That meant universal messages."

KEY NOTES

Richie was inspired to write this song by a speech his father gave at his parents' 37th wedding anniversary party. The speech made Richie realize that he should thank his wife for all of her support.

What You Won't Do for Love
BOBBY CALDWELL

Bobby Caldwell started signing when he was just a kid, but it took him a while to break into the big time. He did just that with "What You Won't Do for Love," which reached No. 9 in 1979. Thanks to Caldwell's smooth R&B stylings on this song, as well as the jazzy ballads that rounded out the parent album, *Bobby Caldwell,* fans were surprised to learn that this soul brother had blue eyes and blonde hair. The way he croons "Got a thing for you and I can't let go" in this single calls to mind Bill Withers, not Barry Manilow. It seems other musicians had a thing for this song, as well. The single has been covered by more than 70 artists, from Natalie Cole to Michael Bolton, and it was even sampled by Tupac Shakur *(left)* and Notorious B.I.G.

In 1998, 2Pac had a posthumous No. 2 rap hit with "Do For Love," which sampled this song.

🌐 BOBBY'S WORLD

Caldwell's parents were singers. In fact, they hosted one of the first television musical variety shows. Caldwell got his  first taste of the stage at age four when he performed "Zippity Doo Dah" at one of his father's shows. At age 12, he began studying piano and guitar. In the late 1960s, Caldwell spent two years touring as a guitarist for Little Richard *(left)*. Caldwell returned home to Florida in the mid-'70s and signed to TK Records. At the time, the label's roster included disco stars like KC and the Sunshine Band and Anita Ward. Caldwell's blend of blue-eyed soul and sophisticated jazz definitely brought a different sound to TK's Clouds label. In addition to the success of "What You Won't Do for Love," Caldwell also cracked the R&B Top 40 with "Can't Say Goodbye," "My Flame" and "Coming Down From Love."

🎤 JAZZ MAN

After TK went bankrupt, Caldwell was without a recording contract for nearly two years. He signed with Polydor and released two albums with the label. In the late '80s, Caldwell scored as a songwriter. His roster of hits includes "What Kind of Man Would I Be" for Chicago and "The Next Time I Fall," a No. 1 single for Peter Cetera *(above)* and Amy Grant. Caldwell's own recordings became immensely popular in Japan. He and his manager eventually formed Sin-Drome Records to release his material in the U.S. His 1999 release, *Come Rain or Come Shine (left)*, made the Top 10 on the jazz chart.

KEY NOTES

In the late '90s, Caldwell appeared as Frank Sinatra in a Las Vegas musical revue, The Rat Pack Is Back, coproduced by former teen idol David Cassidy (right).

Do That to Me One More Time
CAPTAIN & TENNILLE

It is pretty obvious what "Do That to Me One More Time" is about, but in the hands of Captain & Tennille, this is no stereotypical suggestive love song. The emphasis is less on the heat of passion generated when boy meets girl than on the sense of fulfillment that can be found in a long-term, loving relationship. Taken from the *Make Your Move* album, this song was a chart-topper in 1980 for the happily married couple of Daryl "Captain" Dragon and Toni Tennille.

CHANGING TRENDS

For their eight Top 20 hits between 1975 and 1980, Captain & Tennille—often backed by Toni's sisters Melissa and Louisa *(right)*—rarely deviated from upbeat, tender ballads. But with the onset of disco and punk music, their chart popularity waned. The pair stopped singing together full time in 1984, and Tennille pursued a solo career.

MEETING OF MINDS

Dragon met Tennille at a production of *Mother Earth*, a musical Tennille had cowritten, in 1971. Soon after, the pair toured with the Beach Boys, with Dragon on keyboards and Tennille singing backup. Beach Boy Mike Love dubbed Dragon "Captain Keyboard" because of the naval officer's hat he always wore.

MARRIED WITH HITS

Dragon, the son of Hollywood conductor Carmen Dragon *(left, far left, Daryl far right)*, and Tennille were struck by Cupid's arrow as they toured the U.S. to promote their first, self-financed single, "The Way I Want to Touch You." They were married on Valentine's Day in 1975. The following year, with their career on track, they played at a White House dinner for Queen Elizabeth II *(right, with President Ford)*. In 1995, the duo released *Twenty Years of Romance*, as a celebration of their love.

KEY NOTES

The same week that this song topped the singles chart, Tennille could also be heard on the No. 1 album in the country—she was an unlikely contributor to Pink Floyd's The Wall.

Lost in Your Eyes
DEBBIE GIBSON

Debbie Gibson had her second No. 1 hit in 1989 with the ballad "Lost in Your Eyes." On the strength of this single, her sophomore album, *Electric Youth*, also reached the top spot and stayed there for five weeks. This achievement made Gibson the first teenager to simultaneously top both charts since Little Stevie Wonder did it in 1963.

 ## CHILD PRODIGY

Born on Aug. 31, 1970, Debbie Gibson seemed destined for success from age five, when she began piano lessons with the same teacher who had taught her fellow Long Islander—and idol—Billy Joel *(below, with Gibson)*. After

winning $1,000 in a songwriting contest at age 12, Gibson found a manager, and soon had a full-blown recording studio in her garage. Gibson had already recorded more than 100 songs by 1986, when her demo tape got her a deal with Atlantic Records—while she was still in high school.

LESS IS MORE

Although "Lost in Your Eyes" was the first single from
Gibson's second album, it had been in the singer's repertoire
for a while. She wrote the song when her first album was out,
and performed it on her first tour. Positive reaction from fans
guaranteed the song a spot on Gibson's sophomore outing.
Like her previous No. 1, "Foolish Beat," this was a simple

ballad. "That's just the way it evolved," Gibson *(above, in her home studio)* explained.
"…if you have a strong song, you should let it speak for itself and not overproduce it."

BROADWAY-BOUND

As a teen star, Gibson used her perky, girl-next-door look to her full advantage. But in the
early 1990s, she sought to move beyond her teenybopper image, which no longer earned
her an automatic berth on the charts. In 1993, she released *Body Mind Soul,* with songs

and a video intended to present a more adult, even sultry
image—she even insisted on being called Deborah. But
Gibson's most recent successes have come on the musical
stage, in the U.S. and British productions of such shows
as *Les Miserables, Grease (left, with Craig McLachlan),
Funny Girl* and *Beauty and the Beast.*

KEY NOTES

*Gibson's wholesome image made her a target
of satire. In 1989, gonzo rocker Mojo Nixon
released "Debbie Gibson Is Pregnant with My
Two-Headed Love Child," with a video that starred
Winona Ryder (right, with Nixon) as Gibson.*

More Than Words
EXTREME

Forget sweet nothings: In Extreme's hymn to the power of physical touch, "All you have to do is close your eyes and just reach out your hands." Better known as funk rockers, the band revealed its gentler side on this 1991 hit, with a simple acoustic guitar backing the close harmonies of singer Gary Cherone and guitarist Nuno Bettencourt. The song, from Extreme's second album, *Pornograffiti*, touched a chord. Listeners appreciated its sincerity and sent the single all the way to No. 1.

GROUP DECISION

Cherone and drummer Paul Geary played in a band called Dream, while guitarist Bettencourt was in a rival outfit called Sinful. Cherone and Bettencourt met one night when their respective bands were fighting over dressing rooms at a gig. But the two hit it off, and the singer asked the guitarist to work with him—without even hearing him play. The band's lineup was completed by bassist Pat Badger, who had been working in a music store where he was making custom-built guitars.

FROM JOCK TO ROCK

Bettencourt was hesitant about taking up the guitar. He says: "As a kid, I wanted nothing to do with music. I…loved sports, especially hockey and soccer." That all changed when his brother gave him a guitar when Nuno was in his teens. Before long, he was emulating one of his guitar heroes, Eddie Van Halen *(left)*. Ironically, after leaving Extreme, bandmate Cherone became lead singer for Van Halen in 1996.

PORCH SONG

Cherone and Bettencourt wrote "More Than Words" while sitting on the front porch at Cherone's mother's house. They composed the simplistic song with cars and other sounds from the neighborhood in the background. The duo decided to record the track just the way they had played it that day. "I was sure the record company would want to add drums and this big production," Cherone recalled. "But no one said anything."

KEY NOTES

In 1991, Extreme's manager, Arma Andon, insured Bettencourt's fingers for $5 million after the guitarist injured them in a basketball game.

We're All Alone
RITA COOLIDGE

Rita Coolidge's plea to "Let it all begin" in the Boz Scaggs-penned hit "We're All Alone" proved prophetic. The song's rise to No. 7 placed Coolidge in the Top 10 for the second time in 1977 and helped jump-start her solo career. Only months earlier, her cover of Jackie Wilson's "(Your Love Keeps Lifting Me) Higher and Higher" reached No. 2.

HE'S THE BOZ

Singer-songwriter Boz Scaggs *(below)* got his start when he joined the Marksmen, friend Steve Miller's group, in high school. Later, after touring Europe with his own band, Scaggs reunited with his friend in the Steve Miller Band. Then, in 1969, Scaggs started his acclaimed solo career, which hit its peak in 1976 with the multi-platinum album *Silk Degrees*.

🌐 BORN TO SING

Rita Coolidge, whose father was a Baptist minister, got her musical training in the church choir. Then, as a teenager, she recorded radio jingles with her sister Priscilla. In 1971, after two years of singing backup for the likes of Joe Cocker, Eric Clapton and Stephen Stills, Coolidge went solo. But her career didn't take off until the 1977 release of her *Anytime...Anywhere (far right)*, the parent album of "We're All Alone." And though she continues to record—she hit the Top 40 with "All Time High," the theme from the 1983 James Bond movie *Octopussy (poster above)*—*Anytime* and its hits remain the commercial apex of her career.

KEY NOTES

Coolidge's brother-in-law, Booker T. Jones (right), of Booker T. and the MG's, lent his vocal talents to Anytime...Anywhere.

🎤 MUSICAL MUSE

In 1973, Coolidge married musician and actor Kris Kristofferson *(above, with their daughter Casey)*. During their six years together, the two teamed up as a country act and won two Grammys. Prior to marrying, Coolidge had been involved with Steven Stills of Crosby, Stills and Nash, who wrote several songs that were inspired by her. Another ex-boyfriend on whom she left her mark was Leon Russell, who wrote "Delta Lady"—a minor hit for Joe Cocker—about Coolidge.

You and I

EDDIE RABBITT AND CRYSTAL GAYLE

Eddie Rabbitt and Crystal Gayle had both achieved solo success before they came together to record the bittersweet ballad "You and I" in 1982. And sometimes two heads are better than one: When this single reached No. 1 on the country chart and No. 7 on the pop chart early the next year, both Rabbitt and Gayle enjoyed one of the biggest hits of their careers.

Gayle with Loretta Lynn (center) and their mother.

 ## COUNTRY COUSINS

Rabbitt and Gayle were both raised on country music, albeit under very different circumstances. Rabbitt, the son of Irish immigrants, was born in Brooklyn, and raised in East Orange, N.J. Gayle, born Brenda Gayle Webb, was country music royalty almost from birth. She began singing in sister Loretta Lynn's touring band as a teenager. It was Lynn who gave Gayle her stage name. But her talent and distinctive mane quickly brought Gayle recognition when she struck out on her own in the 1970s.

COUNTRIFIED POP

Prior to making their mark on the pop chart, both Rabbitt and Gayle *(below)* had successful careers in country music. Gayle first crossed over in 1977 when "Don't It Make My Brown Eyes Blue" peaked at No. 2 on the pop chart. In 1980, Rabbitt hit the Top 5 on the country and pop charts with "Drivin' My Life Away," from the soundtrack to the movie *Roadie*. But he is best known for "I Love a Rainy Night," which went to No. 1 on the pop chart the following year. In 1982, both artists built on their crossover success, as Gayle joined Rabbitt to record "You and I" for his *Radio Romance* album.

RUN, RABBITT, RUN

Rabbitt spent the 1960s trying to make it as a songwriter in Nashville, where he palled around with other up-and-coming outsiders like Kris Kristofferson *(below, with Rabbitt),* Billy Swan and Larry Gatlin. He got his first big break in 1970 when Elvis Presley recorded his "Kentucky Rain" and made

it a Top 20 hit. "That legitimized me," Rabbitt told a reporter. "The doors that had been closed to me before were opened." In 1976, he scored his first country chart-topper with "Drinking My Baby (Off My Mind)." Rabbitt would follow up that success with an amazing 16 more No. 1 country hits during his career. After his son Timmy died of liver disease in 1985, Rabbitt pulled away from the touring grind to spend more time with his family and on charitable work. He died of lung cancer in 1998, at age 56.

KEY NOTES

Rabbitt's "American Boy" was a favorite of U.S. troops during the Gulf War. Bob Dole (right) used the song at rallies during his 1996 presidential bid.

Tonight I Celebrate My Love
PEABO BRYSON & ROBERTA FLACK

Peabo Bryson and Roberta Flack own two of the richest voices in music. Give them any song and they can make it sound special. Give them a beautiful ballad like this one, and they will soar to even greater heights. Singing together for more than three years provided the duo with a closeness that gave "Tonight I Celebrate My Love" an extra emotional intensity and propelled it to No. 16 in 1983.

PEABO'S STORY

Although Bryson has been in the music business almost as long as Flack, he has spent less time in the spotlight. Born in 1951, Bryson grew up on a farm in South Carolina and joined his first band at 14. From 1968, he toured with soul group Moses Dillard and the Tex-Town Display. Throughout the '70s, he worked solo and with other bands and appeared regularly on the R&B chart.

GETTING TOGETHER

In the early 1970s, Roberta Flack made a name for herself with soulful ballads like "The First Time Ever I Saw Your Face" and "Killing Me Softly with His Song"—both No. 1 singles. She often sang with college friend and R&B singer-songwriter Donny Hathaway *(right)*, before his suicide in 1979. The grief-stricken Flack took a year off after Hathaway's death, before returning to work with Bryson as her new duetting partner.

FROM THE HIT FACTORY

This song was written by two of the best hit-makers in the business, Gerry Goffin and Michael Masser. Goffin, along with wife Carole King, had emerged as one of the most prolific and successful songwriters of the 1960s. Goffin and King cowrote more than 100 hits before they divorced in 1967. Goffin later teamed up with Masser to write a pair of No. 1 hits: Diana Ross' "Do You Know Where You're Going To" and Whitney Houston's "Saving All My Love for You."

Gerry Goffin (bottom row, center, with King on right) *was a graduate of the Brill Building "Factory."*

KEY NOTES

In the 1990s, Bryson had a pair of huge hits with duets from Disney films. He teamed with Celine Dion (right) for the theme to Beauty and the Beast *and with Regina Belle for "A Whole New World" from* Aladdin.

Baby, Come to Me

PATTI AUSTIN (A DUET WITH JAMES INGRAM)

Love can change your life, but only if you seize the fleeting moment. Such is the sentiment at the heart of the Quincy Jones-produced "Baby, Come to Me," a No. 1 single for Patti Austin and James Ingram in 1983. Building on a jazz-influenced melody with mellow guitars and a languid electric piano, the duet sees Austin and Ingram trade impassioned, enchanting vocals as they reveal how wonderful they make each other feel.

SOAP OPERA SONG

Originally released in 1982, this single topped the chart in the following year after it was used in the ABC soap opera *General Hospital* as the theme song for characters Luke and Holly *(right)*. In 1984, Christopher Cross' ballad "Think of Laura" broke into the Top 10 after it was used as the theme song for Luke and his long lost love, Laura.

PROLIFIC PATTI

Born in 1948, Austin first sang in public at New York's Apollo Theatre when she was five. After releasing several jazz albums in the '70s, Austin got her big break after appearing on Quincy Jones'

Grammy-winning album *The Dude*. Jones *(left, on right, with Austin and Ingram)* signed her to his Qwest label and paired her with Ingram for this hit.

DOUBLING UP

Like Austin, Ingram is probably best known for his collaborations with other artists. As a songwriter, he teamed up with Quincy Jones to write "P.Y.T. (Pretty Young Thing)" for Michael Jackson's classic *Thriller* album. The year after "Baby, Come to Me" was released, Ingram and former Doobie Brother Michael McDonald joined forces on "Yah Mo B There," a Top 20 hit. In 1986, Ingram duetted with Linda Ronstadt on the No. 2 hit "Somewhere Out There," from the animated film *An American Tail (above)*.

In his search to find his family, he discovered America.

KEY NOTES

Austin and Ingram teamed up again in 1983 on "How Do You Keep the Music Playing," the theme for Best Friends, a film starring Goldie Hawn and Burt Reynolds.

Reunited
PEACHES & HERB

On love, there's nothing more satisfying than making up after an argument. The relief and fun of getting back together are both captured in Peaches & Herb's "Reunited," a No. 1 hit in 1979. Audibly harking back to Motown's 1960s heyday, this is a good old-fashioned love song from the duo dubbed "the Sweethearts of Soul." This platinum track gave listeners a soothing break from the pumping disco and new wave music that ruled the airwaves and the charts in the late '70s.

RETAIL THERAPY

Producer and songwriter Freddie Perren—who has worked with the Jackson 5 and New Edition—played a major part in Peaches & Herb's success. As a teenager, Herb worked in a record store; his friend Perren worked in a shop around the corner. More than a decade later, the one-time retail assistants were "reunited" in the studio, with Perren cowriting this song and producing the parent album, *2 Hot!*

LUCKY LINDA

Washington-born Linda Greene *(below)* was a model before taking a chance as a

singer. She says: "I bumped into producer Van McCoy and told him I...wished I could get into the record business. I thought I was ready to handle something like that." McCoy renamed her "Peaches" and teamed her up with Herb Fame.

 ARRESTED BY MUSIC

The duo that recorded "Reunited" was actually the third incarnation of Peaches & Herb. The first began in 1965 when singer Herb Fame, born Herbert Feemster in 1942, was introduced to singer Francine "Peaches" Barker by producer Van McCoy *(left)*. The duo recorded several hits before Barker took time off and was replaced by Marlene Mack. Herb soon hung up his microphone and joined the Washington, D.C. police force. But after working the beat for several years, Herb decided he missed his original beat—in the recording studio—and left the force to restart his music career, this time with Linda Greene as his Peaches.

KEY NOTES

In 1979, Peaches & Herb became the first African-American recording act to perform live in China, as part of a TV special with Bob Hope (right).

Credits & Acknowledgements

PICTURE CREDITS

Page 2: (L) Corbis (H.Diltz), (BR) London Features International Ltd. (Celebrity Photo/J.Paschal)
Page 3: (TL) London Features International Ltd., (CR) Idols (P.Cox), (BL) Redferns **Page 4:** (BL) Corbis (L.Goldsmith), (R) Retna (D.Redfern) **Page 5:** (TL) Retna Michael Ochs Archives, (RC) Retna (V.Oakland), (BL) Globe Photos (F.Barrett), (BR) Everett Collection **Page 6:** (B) Retna (D.Redfern) **Page 7:** (TL) BMI Archives, (BC) Globe Photos (Herm Lewis & Associates) **Page 8:** (R) Pictorial Press **Page 9:** (C) Pictorial Press, (RC) Retna (K.Garner), (TL) Retna (R.Matheu) **Page 10:** (B) Redferns (Michael Ochs Archives) **Page 11:** (BC) Corbis (M.Gerber), (TL) Pictorial Press, (RC) Redferns **Page 12:** (BL) Redferns (C.Modu), (R) Courtesy of Sin-Drome Records **Page 13:** (TL) Corbis, (TR) Pictorial Press (R.Reiner), (BR) Retna (S.Granitz) **Page 14:** (B) Corbis **Page 15:** (RC) Corbis, (T) Corbis, (LC) Image Bank (Archive Photos/Express Newspapers **Page 16:** (BL) London Features International Ltd. (K.Mazur), (R) Retna (S.Double) **Page 17:** (TR) Star File (C.Pulin), (BL) Globe Photos (D.G.Morgan), (BR) London Features International Ltd. (K.Mazur) **Page 18:** (B) Rex Features (D.Hogan)

Page 19: (BC) Corbis, (TR) Getty/TSI (A.Sacks) **Page 20:** (BR) London Features International Ltd. (N.Elgar), (L) Redferns (D.Redfern) **Page 21:** (TL) Ronald Grant Archive (Eon Productions), (BC) Redferns (Glenn A. Baker Archives), (TR) Rex Features **Page 22:** (TL) Globe Photos (L.McAfee), (BR) Globe Photos (R.Dominguez) **Page 23:** (LC) Retna (L.McAfee), (TR) Globe Photos (T.Rodriguez), (BC) Associated Press **Page 24:** (BR) Retna (S.Weiner) **Page 25:** (BR) Colorific (G.Schachmes/Regards), (TR,TL) Redferns **Page 26:** (B) London Features International Ltd. (Imperial Press) **Page 27:** (C) Corbis, (RC) Ronald Grant Archive, (BL) London Features International Ltd. (L.McAfee) **Page 28:** (R) Redferns **Page 29:** (T) Redferns (G.A.Baker), (BL,BR) Rex Features

Artwork: **John See**

The Publisher has made every effort to obtain the copyright holders' permission for the use of the pictures which have been supplied by the sources listed above, and undertakes to rectify any accidental omissions.